T0348147

THIS ALBUM BELONGS TO

_____

WHITE STAR PUBLISHERS

CONTENTS

THIS IS HOW MOM
AND DAD IMAGINED ME

BEFORE I ARRIVED

My parents found out about my arrival when

This is what Mom told Dad:

This is how Dad reacted:

The date of my expected birth was

IN MOM'S BIG BELLY

My parents heard my heartbeat for the first time
_____

Mom felt me kick for the first time
_____

While waiting for me, Mom always had a craving for
_____

_____

My family made important preparations before my arrival, such as:
_____

_____

_____

_____

_____

The first ultrasound

PHOTOS OF MOM AND HER BIG BELLY

📷 Pictures

MY FAMILY

Mom's name is
_____

Her dream for me is
_____
_____

Dad's name is
_____

His dream for me is
_____
_____

The other members of my family
_____
_____
_____

MY FAMILY TREE

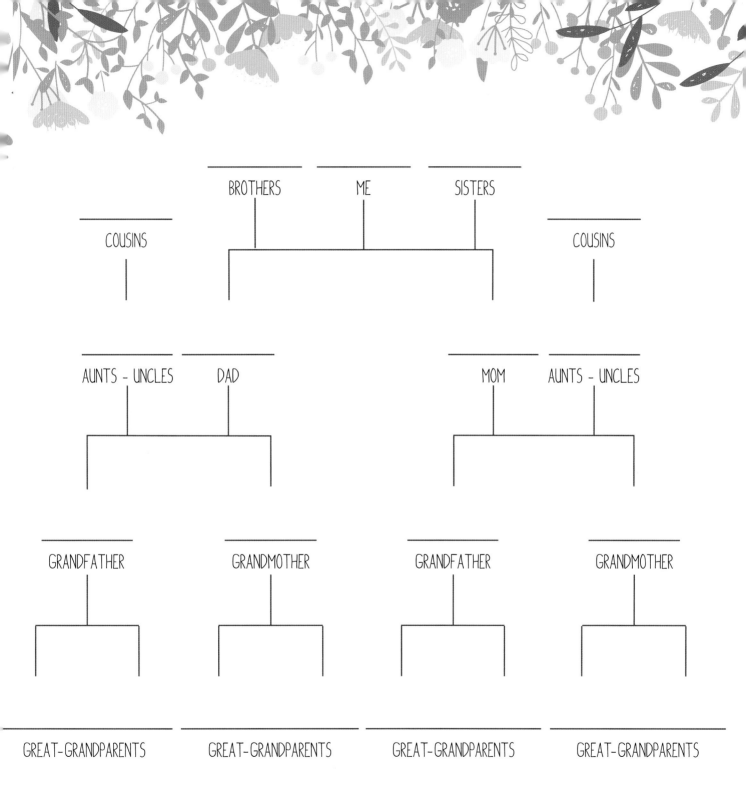

BROTHERS   ME   SISTERS

COUSINS

COUSINS

AUNTS - UNCLES   DAD

MOM   AUNTS - UNCLES

GRANDFATHER   GRANDMOTHER   GRANDFATHER   GRANDMOTHER

GREAT-GRANDPARENTS   GREAT-GRANDPARENTS   GREAT-GRANDPARENTS   GREAT-GRANDPARENTS

📷 Pictures of me

I AM BORN!

I was born on

At _____ a.m./p.m.

I weighed _____ pounds/kilogrammes

I was _____ inches/centimeters tall

I was born in

Mom and Dad describe my first day like this:

The most vivid recollection of that day

WHAT THEY SAID ABOUT ME...

Mom's first words were

_____

_____

Dad's first words were

_____

The reactions of my siblings, cousins, grandparents, uncles, aunts and friends:

_____

I also received best wishes from

_____

_____

_____

_____

_____

_____

PRECIOUS MEMENTOS

A LOCK OF MY HAIR

MY HOSPITAL ID BRACELET

📷 Pictures of me

MY NAME

Mom's and Dad's favorite names were

The name they decided on is

They chose this name because

My name means

My nickname is

They call me this because

MY PORTRAIT

My eyes are _____

My hair is _____

Distinguishing marks: _____

_____

How I take after Mom _____

_____

How I take after Dad _____

_____

They say I also look like _____

_____

_____

_____

📷 Pictures of me

📷 Pictures of me

WELCOME HOME!

The date I arrived at home

My first address:

During the trip, I

Waiting for me at home

As soon as I was inside, I

MY PHOTOS

SWEET DREAMS!

My first night at home I slept _____ hours

And my parents slept _____ hours

That first night they thought _____

_____

To fall asleep I need _____

_____

My favorite lullaby is _____

_____

The position I sleep in _____

_____

I can't fall asleep if _____

_____

_____

_____

Pictures of me

WAKE UP, SLEEPYHEAD!

Am I an early riser or a sleepyhead?

This is how I tell everyone I'm awake:

As soon as I open my eyes, I immediately want

IT'S TIME TO EAT!

My first solid food

Mom's recipes

My favorite dish

I really don't like

I used a spoon all by myself when I was

Mom's secret recipe

MY PHOTOS

📷 Pictures of me

IT'S BATH TIME

My first time in water
_____
_____
_____
_____

My reactions
_____
_____
_____
_____

In the water I enjoy
_____
_____
_____
_____

MY PHOTOS

I GROW SO FAST

1 MONTH — height   weight

3 MONTHS — height   weight

6 MONTHS — height   weight

9 MONTHS — height   weight

1 YEAR — height   weight

The first little tooth erupted when I was

AT THE DOCTOR

My pediatrician

During the first visit, I

My blood group

The first time I got sick

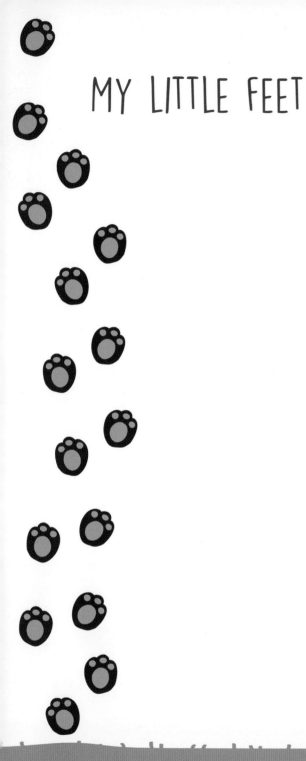

MY LITTLE FEET

MY LITTLE HANDS

DISCOVERING THE WORLD!

The first family stroll was
_____
_____
_____

This was my reaction:
_____
_____
_____

The persons I met said the following about me:
_____
_____
_____
_____
_____

My favorite places are
_____
_____
_____

My family's first vacation
_____
_____
_____
_____
_____
_____
_____
_____
_____

MY PHOTOS

THE FIRST TIME THAT...

I recognized Mom and Dad

I raised my head

I smiled

I slept all night long

I clapped my hands

I discovered my tiny feet

I sat down all by myself

I traveled in a car

I traveled by train, plane or ship

I saw the sea

I touched the snow

47

TAKING MY FIRST STEPS

I began to crawl
_____

_____

_____

_____

I stood up all by myself
_____

_____

_____

_____

_____

_____

_____

I began to walk with some help

I walked for the first time all by myself

MY PHOTOS

I LIKE THIS SO MUCH!

My favorite toy

My favorite book

I smile every time I hear this song

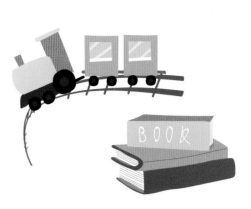

The thing that makes me happy most of all

The thing that makes me angry most of all

What soothes me

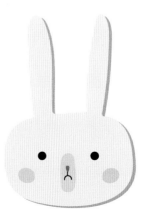

MY FIRST BIRTHDAY

The date and venue of the party

The guests

The presents I received

A special recollection

1

MY PHOTOS

LOOK WHO'S TALKING!

My first word was

The first time I said "Mama" and "Dada"

Here are my very own words that I used to indicate certain objects

Ma-ma
Da-da Ba-ba
La-la

THE FIRST TIME THAT...

I built a tower
_____

_____

_____

I tried to get dressed on my own
_____

_____

_____

_____

I ate on my own
_____

_____

_____

_____

_____

_____

I threw a ball in the air

I jumped

My new experiences

MY SECOND BIRTHDAY

The date and venue of the party

The guests

The presents I received

A special recollection

MY PHOTOS

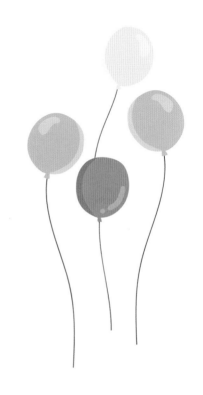

THE FIRST TIME THAT...

I stopped wearing diapers

_____

I drew a circle

_____

I recognized colors

_____

I counted up to 5

_____

I brushed my teeth myself

_____

_____

_____

I rode a tricycle

I dressed on my own

I used my own name

A new experience

MY THIRD BIRTHDAY

The date and venue of the party

_____

The guests

_____

_____

The presents I received

_____

_____

_____

A special recollection

_____

_____

3

_____

_____

_____

MY PHOTOS

THE FIRST TIME THAT...

I drew a picture of an animal

_____

_____

_____

I went to a friend's party

_____

_____

_____

_____

_____

_____

_____

_____

I chose my clothes in the morning

I wrote my own name

I stopped using a pacifier

AT NURSERY SCHOOL

How I reacted the first day at nursery school

My teachers are called

My new friends are called:

MY BEST FRIEND

MY FRIENDS

My friends' names are:

_____

_____

_____

The games I like to play with them

_____

_____

The game I like the best

_____

_____

The game I dislike the most

_____

_____

_____

THREE UNFORGETTABLE YEARS

The moments over these years that Mom and Dad will never forget

_____

_____

_____

_____

_____

_____

_____

_____

_____

_____

_____

_____

Graphic Design
Paola Piacco

Photo Credits
All photographs are by Supidcha Wongwichaichana/123RF

WHITE STAR PUBLISHERS

WS White Star Publishers® is a registered trademark
property of White Star s.r.l.

© 2021 White Star s.r.l.
Piazzale Luigi Cadorna, 6 - 20123 Milan, Italy
www.whitestar.it

ISBN 978-88-544-1662-8
1 2 3 4 5 6   25 24 23 22 21

Printed in China